When Evil
Seems to Triumph Over Good

Father,
Sometimes I Don't Know
What to Pray

JEFFREY CAMPBELL

When Evil Seems To Triumph Over Good Father, Sometimes I Don't Know What to Pray
© Copyright 2001, Jeffrey Campbell
All rights reserved

Published by: **Tau publishing**
Printed in U.S.A.

Visit us at: **www.Tau-publishing.org**
For re-orders and other publications as well as our daily updated
Scriptural reflections and meditations.

ISBN 0-9719921-1-8
First Edition November 2004

About the Cover
Perhaps the most powerful image depicting the Way of the Cross is the 13th
Station. Mary holding the lifeless body of Jesus has inspired artists
for almost two thousand years. Even more powerful than the 14th Station
where Jesus is laid in the tomb, the moment Jesus is laid in the arms of
His mother Mary, brings the finality of Jesus' death upon her.

Prior to that moment there was still hope. Before that heart wrenching
moment there was still the possibility that Jesus would come down from
the cross in triumphant victory. Instead it appeared that evil had won.
It appeared that death was victorious. It appeared that it was the end.

For My Mother

Introduction

*Father help me to understand
why there is so much evil in this world
and why it seems to be triumphing over Good.*

Evil has been with us since the serpent tempted Eve in the garden. It has flourished from the moment she succumbed to the delicious fruit. It began its work with the cunning words from the one whose only mission is to bring about the destruction of the souls our Father in heaven desires to bring back to Him. The work of satan has not diminished since Adam and Eve. The enemy is trying constantly to gain souls for his purpose, enticing them at every moment with his lies.

The greatest gift God has given man is free will. Since the time our heavenly Father placed Adam and Eve in the garden, we have been free to make whatever choices we wished. However, just as with Adam and Eve, there are consequences to the choices we make. The choices, good or bad, have an effect not only on ourselves but on others.

The forces of evil have seemingly been growing in recent times. More and more people are activating their free will for the glory of the evil one and not for the greater glory of God's Kingdom. It appears we are moving into a time where evil is overtaking the good in this world and perhaps may triumph. Rest assured, however, the evil one has already been defeated. His demise came when our Lord stretched out His arms upon His cross, died, and two days later rose from His tomb. At that moment our Lord claimed victory forever. **"Where, O death, is your victory? Where, death, is your sting?"**[1]

If Satan and the forces of evil have been defeated, then why does evil seem to be growing in these times? Christ's death on His cross ransomed us from our sins. His death didn't take away the free will of man; it only made it more significant. We can choose to accept what Jesus purchased for us through His crucifixion or reject it by freely aligning ourselves with the evil one.

We have the reassurance of eternal life. We have the promise of salvation through Christ's suffering, death and resurrection. We have the truth. The enemy has the truth. Satan, however, still does not accept it anymore than when he was cast out of heaven with a third of the angels. All of this makes our free will even more important. The prince of darkness is angry. He is working frantically in every way possible to gain souls. He also knows the time is approaching when our Lord will return in all His glory. **"He will wipe every tear from their eyes. There will be no more death, or crying or pain, for the old order of things has passed away."**[2] When this comes to pass, evil will be no more. It will be locked away forever in the pit of the underworld. All those who took seriously their free will and the words given to them from our heavenly Father through His Son Jesus Christ will live forever with Him in eternity.

Still, knowing that evil has been defeated makes it no less easy to fully understand *why* it manifests itself so violently around us. It doesn't make it any easier to accept, despite knowing that one day our Lord will return and evil will be no more.

There are varying opinions as to how we should combat the evil around us. What position should we take

---

1   1 *Corinthians* 15:55
2   *Revelations* 21:4

against it? Most often when evil is so perverse, so violent; all we can do is place ourselves in the presence of our Father and ask for His mercy. Sometimes, the only answer to the evil around us is to pray. Yet when such evil is cast around us, it is difficult to know just what to pray and whom to pray for.

It is not always easy to place ourselves in a prayerful state of mind when evil has taken over our lives and the world in which we live. It is difficult to pray what is truly in our hearts when we cannot always find the words to ask our Father to help us. Our heavenly Father already knows what is in our hearts before we ask Him; yet, it is comforting when we can offer up words to Him asking for His intercession for ourselves and for those for whom we are praying.

This book was written to give us prayers when no prayer can be easily pulled from our hearts. These prayers are meant to open us to our Father's love, guidance and protection. They are to help us feel as if we are playing an active part when sometimes there is little we can really do on our own. Yet, our prayers to the Father do so much and mean so much. Not only do they mean so much for those for whom we are praying, but for ourselves as well.

These are prayers asking Him for an *understanding* of and the *patience to endure* evil manifestations. They are prayers that allow the *emotions* within us to be safely released; prayers that ask Him for *direction* when we do not know which way to turn; and prayers petitioning our Father to give us the *strength and courage* to continue in the face of uncertainty. They are prayers leading us to *forgiveness*, freeing us to move beyond the evil around us. They are prayers helping us to see the souls around us as true *brothers and sisters* in Christ. And finally, they are prayers of *hope and thanksgiving* offered to our Father for whatever circumstances we find ourselves in. These prayers are supplications to our Father asking Him to show us the goodness that is turned from even the worst manifestations of evil.

There is no set pattern to prayer. There is no one prayer that is better than another. All prayer that flows from the heart is good. All prayer, whether it comes from our own heart or is read from a book, is good. All prayer that is offered with a humble heart is heard in the highest realms of heaven. Every prayer that flows from a loving, truthful heart is answered by God. We may not always get the answer we are searching for, but we *will* get an answer. It may not be what we want, but it will be what we *need*. At times when evil manifests itself around us, we do not always know what is needed or what direction we are supposed to take. Rest assured, our Father in heaven knows.

As we invoke these prayers from our heart, we place our trust in God. We have faith that He has everything under control, even when evil seems to have taken all control away.

For a while it seemed the evil of those who crucified Jesus had defeated the Goodness sent to us from our Father. However, how much greater is our God that He can overcome even death itself. The CROSS is a constant reminder of this triumphant victory. No more would it represent death but life itself.

UNDERSTANDING AND PATIENCE

*Therefore
we will not fear,
though the earth
give way.*

Psalm 46:2

While he was speaking, yet another messenger came and said, "Your sons and daughters were feasting and drinking wine at the oldest brother's house, when suddenly a mighty wind swept in from the desert and struck the four corners of the house. It collapsed on them and they are dead, and I am the only one who has escaped to tell you!"

Job 1:18-19

When our world is literally crumbling before us, we look to our Father in heaven with tears in our eyes and sorrow in our hearts. We ask, "Why Lord?" As we open ourselves to the Father, we try earnestly to understand what has happened in our lives and in the world around us. We patiently await an answer, but often the answers are not quick in coming. Our faith is tested, but part of our faith is perseverance in times of adversity, something not easily understood.

Father, Help Me to Understand

My heart aches heavenly Father,
please help me.
All I see around me at this moment is heartache, confusion
and souls who are suffering.
Show me the light that waits
at the end of this dark moment.
I know You are here Father.
I know You are in me,
with me and around me.
Why can't I feel You at this moment?
Father, I don't know what to pray.
I can't find the words to ask You for help.
Read my heart, feel the pain I am feeling
and please Father, comfort these afflictions.
Comfort this overwhelming sense of loss.
Father, help me to understand.

And when Jesus cried out again in a loud voice, he gave up His Spirit.

Matthew 27:50

We can visualize our Lord hanging on His cross, but until we really stop to comprehend what it must have been like, we cannot fully understand what He had to endure. Now as we look at our own suffering and the afflictions of others, as we sense and feel the pain first hand, we begin to understand just what our Lord endured for each of us upon His cross. As we come to a better understanding of His suffering through our own and that of those around us, we are saddened by not having taken the time to truly understand what He experienced.

I Am Sorry Lord

I know You suffered on Your cross Lord.
The pain You must have felt is beyond comprehension.
I never truly realized this before.
As I see so much suffering around me,
in each face, each broken hope,
I can begin to see the pain You felt.
As this suffering touches my own life,
it becomes even more of a reality.
I am sorry Lord
I didn't look at Your wounds this way before,
yet I don't know if I could have.
It is so painful seeing You suffer.
I know this is what You lived on that dark Friday afternoon.
I am sorry Lord for what You had to endure.
Your patience as You were crucified
is a testimony to the love You have for us,
and each moment You patiently endured Your suffering
made that love only more visible.
Lord I need that patience now.

"My God, My God, why have You forsaken Me."
                                        Matthew 27:46

Jesus endured His suffering upon His cross. He felt the pain throughout His body from the nails that pierced every corner of His flesh. As He cried out and looked toward His Father and breathed His last. He felt alone. He felt abandoned in His suffering. He could no longer feel the presence of the One who always felt so close to Him. Despite this feeling of abandonment, Jesus never lost sight of where He was going. He showed us this by looking up toward heaven as he was dying upon His cross. Even when we feel as if we have been abandoned by God, we must stay focused on our eternal reward. We must continue to seek that understanding and never lose sight of where we are going, even when we cannot feel His presence.

Where Are You My God

Where are You?
Why have You left me here alone to endure this pain?
Why can I no longer feel Your presence
as I struggle to understand the evil
that has manifested itself upon this earth?
Why my God have You abandoned me?
Why my heavenly Father have You forsaken me?
You have always been so close.
You have always been at my side.
Now as I am experiencing my deepest hour,
I cannot find You.
Please let me hear Your voice, feel Your presence.
Father let me feel Your gentle hand upon me once more.
If I could just feel your presence,
I know it would be easier to endure what is now upon me.

"A time is coming when anyone who kills you will think he is offering service to God. They will do such things because they have not known the Father or Me."

John 16:2-3

How many times since our Lord spoke these words to His disciples have they come true? Even today, Evil is manifested in this world under the guise of religion. It is difficult to understand those who believe that what they are doing is justified, because they feel God has called them to these actions. Yet, we must be careful our *reactions* do not follow the same thinking.

Your Truth

Heavenly Father,
please help me understand what is happening.
I have read Your words,
I have listened to Your teachings.
Nothing you have taught us allows such actions.
You sent your Son to show us
Your love, Your peace, Your Salvation.
Please send Him once more to us,
so we can clearly understand Your truth.
Heavenly Father,
please help us to know what You expect from us
as we respond to the evil around us.

And no wonder, for satan himself masquerades as an angel of light.

2 Corinthians 11:14

We can never predict God's actions. Even satan, who has far more knowledge than we do, does not know the mind of God. Satan is very clever, but he is nothing in comparison to our heavenly Father. This should give us confidence that when evil strikes out at us, we must understand his victory will not last. Sometimes we just need patience to see the glory of God shine through.

Not Normal Days

Father,
I know in my heart
Your goodness will triumph over evil.
On a normal day,
this is easy to understand and accept,
but these are not normal days.
These are days when my heart aches,
because of the evil brought into this world.
Please heavenly Father,
give me the patience
to await the triumph of your goodness.

EMOTIONS

*Jesus entered the temple
area and drove out all
who were buying and
selling there.
He overturned the table
of the money changers
and the benches of those
selling dove.*

Matthew 21:12

> *When Jesus saw her weeping, and the Jews who had come along with her also weeping, he was deeply moved in spirit and troubled.*
>
> John 11:33

As Jesus looked toward the tomb of His good friend Lazarus, He began to weep. He wept not because He didn't believe Lazarus was in a better place, but because He felt the loss of this dear friend. He also sensed the pain of Martha and Mary. He wept over the brother He loved even though He had the power to raise his decayed body from the tomb. It is good to shed tears for one another. It is a normal human response to our emotions. It is healthy to let those emotions flow through the eyes of our soul. Tears reveal the deep love we have for our brothers and sisters. Tears flow even though our loved ones have gone on to live forever in a place where there are only tears of joy.

Tears

The tears have not stopped flowing Lord
since the loss of those I love.
I know they have gone to a place
far better than where they were,
but I still feel the loss.
I still feel the pain,
not just for those who now rest in your Kingdom,
but for their loved ones left behind.
My brothers and sisters weep along with me
because of the love we have for them.
Just as you raised Lazarus from the tomb,
I know Lord you will raise all those who rest in your peace.
Tears are overflowing for those who have left this world
by all of us who await the day
we will rest in your peace together.

After Jesus said this, He looked toward heaven and prayed.
John 17:1

When Jesus knelt down in the Garden of Gethsemane, He spoke freely from the heart about what He was feeling at that moment. As He petitioned His Father, tears poured from His heart knowing the fate that awaited Him. His emotions overwhelmed Him to the point of sweating blood. As we open our hearts to our Father, as we share with Him our innermost feelings and our deepest fears, we allow our own emotions to emerge from the deepest part of our souls. They are normal human reactions that even Jesus had while He lived His humanity in the Garden. Human emotions reveal to us how much we need our Father in heaven to help us.

These Feelings

Heavenly Father,
my pain, my suffering, runs deep
and can be felt as every breath I take lays heavy upon
my soul.
Father I know I must continue.
I must go forth as you have sent me
to complete the work you desire of me,
just as You sent Your Son forth
from the Garden to the Hill
to fulfill what was long ago spoken by Your prophets.
I know dear Father long before time began You saw this day,
You saw my suffering, my pain.
Forgive me Father for being so weak in these moments.
I need You Father to help me through these feelings,
these emotions,
just as You helped Your Son through His.

"Do not let your hearts be troubled."

John 14:1

It is arduous not to let our heart be troubled when there is so much weighted upon it. It is difficult to place complete trust in God and our Lord when it seems the world is so overcome by evil. Yet, these are times when it is most important not to allow the evil that is present to press down upon our hearts. We must allow our hearts to be free to love, free to give, free to not only trust in God, but in His Son Jesus Christ. We must not let our hearts be troubled to the point they begin to harden or become cold.

My Heart is Heavy

My heart is heavy Lord,
my heart is weighted down by the evil around me.
Please dear God, through Your Son, through His love,
lift this burden from my heart.
Free my heart
so it no longer feels the burden
placed upon it.
Help me heavenly Father to trust in Your power,
to trust in the power of Your Son's cross.
Help me to trust that even though I feel so much upon me
at this moment,
how much greater is Your love,
how much greater is the love of Your Son Jesus Christ.
Please help me to not allow what I am feeling
at this moment
to harden my heart to His love.

DIRECTION

*"But I tell you who hear Me:
love your enemies,
do good to those
who hate you,
bless those who curse you
pray for those who
mistreat you."*

Luke 6:27

Then Jesus said to His disciples, "If anyone would come after me, he must deny himself and take up his cross and follow me."

Matthew 16:24

Are these only *words* we read or recite to ourselves, and then close the bible and move onto something else? Or, do we really live them? Do we truly know what it means when our Lord says to *renounce* ourselves? Do we even *know* what our crosses are? Furthermore, how many of us truly accept them and move forward? Sometimes our crosses have been with us since our beginning, but sometimes they are suddenly placed upon us. Whichever way we have been given them, we must pick them up and move forward—no matter how difficult the task may become.

Our Cross

Lord, none of us have escaped
without one or more crosses being placed upon us.
Some we have carried for a long time,
some, through the actions of others,
have been suddenly thrust upon our shoulders.
What direction do we take Lord,
once we find ourselves carrying these heavy burdens?
Give us the grace Lord Jesus to accept them
no matter how difficult the journey may become.
Lead us Lord as we accept them,
knowing you never give us more
than we can carry.

Again Jesus said, "Peace be with you! As the Father has sent Me, I am sending you."

John 20:21

Sometimes we can work for a long time for peace to come about. It may seem many times like we have not made any progress. But rest assured, even if we have not made progress through our faithfulness to its end, we have not slipped further behind.

The Right Direction

Lord, it seems at times
as if all I am doing is going nowhere.
Grant me the grace Lord Jesus,
to continue
even when I see no outward signs of peace.
All is in Your hands,
All that shall be done
will come about
because of the work You are doing
through the willing vessels
who realize the importance of this task.
Lead us in the right direction Lord,
a direction that leads toward peace
as You so desire it,
as all who follow You so desire it.

At that moment the temple of the curtain was torn in two from top to bottom. The earth shook and the rocks split.
                                        Matthew 27:51

On the third day after our Lord was crucified came that glorious Easter morning. The finality that caused the earth to tremble stilled as *life* overpowered *death*. How distressing it was three days earlier to attempt to see beyond the suffering hanging lifeless upon the wood. One couldn't. The cross had to be lived. Jesus had to *die* upon it before He could *rise* in His glory.

Days of the Cross

Lord, I cannot see past the suffering of Your cross.
I cannot see any light beyond Your arms
stretched out before the world.
The darkness of death
has blackened the afternoon sky,
Yet, with each moment that passes
this part is being lived,
just as it was for Your mother Mary
as she watched you suffer and die.
Soon they will bring you down
and lay you in your tomb
where the light will overpower the darkness
and death will be no more.
Carry us Lord through these days of the cross,
comfort us through each moment as they are lived,
until once more the light returns,
only this time never to fade.

"I pray for them. I am not praying for the world, but for those you have given me, for they are yours."

John 17:9

In the seventeenth chapter of John's gospel, Jesus offered up a prayer to our Father. In that prayer He petitioned Him to protect His disciples from the evil one. In this prayer He was also praying for those who were yet to follow Him. How we feel the necessity for that protection now. We cannot live in this world without divine protection from evil.

Protect Us Father

Protect us Father,
hold us always in Your hand.
Protect us from all evil around us.
Please keep us safely away from his fiery arrows,
guide us through all the snares
he has placed along our path.
Alert us Father,
through Your heavenly angels
of the dangers that could overtake us.
Direct us Father, back to Your kingdom
where we will be away from the evil one forever.

STRENGTH AND COURAGE

An angel from heaven appeared to Him and strengthened Him.

Luke 22:43

"So do not fear, for I am with you; do not be dismayed for I am your God. I will strengthen you and help you."

Isaiah 41:10

"Have no Fear" is one of the most repeated verses in Holy Scripture. Over and over again our Lord repeats these words. Yet, it's difficult not to be fearful when the evil one casts so much around us to cause this fear. Fear is not of God. Our direction should always be away from fear and toward the One who can place true peace within our hearts.

Have No Fear

I don't want to be afraid.
I don't want to wake up each morning
fearful of the day ahead.
Lord, so many times You told your Apostles,
Your followers, "Have no fear."
Place these words Lord into my heart.
Reinforce them in my spirit.
Etch them forever upon my soul,
so fear is permanently replaced by Your peace.

For who is God but Yahweh, who is a rock but our God: this God who girds me with strength, who makes my way free from blame, who makes me as swift as a deer and sets me firmly on the heights, who trains my hands for battle my arms to bend a bow of bronze. You give me your invincible shield, you never cease to listen to me, you give me the strides of a giant, give me ankles that never weaken.

2 Samuel 32-37

Sometimes we have more strength within than we realize, because it is our Father who strengthens us when we need it the most. He never allows more to be placed upon our shoulders than we can carry. It is when we are most tested we must reach deep within for this strength to carry us through.

Inner Strength

Heavenly Father,
I know you have placed within me
the strength to overcome all of the afflictions
brought down upon me.
In my distress,
I can't even find the energy
to call upon my inner strength.
Help me Lord
to reach deep within my soul
to the place of strength
that will sustain me through this suffering.

Carry each others burdens, and in this way you will fulfill the law of Christ.

Galatians 6:2

Oftentimes we have to be strong for others. There are so many who are lacking in their faith who cannot deal with even the slightest sorrow or heartache in their lives. Then when an abundance of pain comes their way, they are overwhelmed—even to the point of losing what little faith they have. The evil one uses these times to overtake a weak soul. It is at this juncture we must help those around us who cannot stand on their own. We must encourage and lift up those who have fallen because their faith has not been able to sustain them.

I Have You Lord

Lord, I can see the toll that
has now been taken by the actions of the evil one.
Give me strength Lord
not only to lift myself up,
but to lift up those around me.
Give me the courage to do what I need to do,
even though my own pain is overwhelming.
I have you Lord,
and for those who have not yet recognized you
I know I may be the only peace they will find.
Please Lord, through me,
touch their
hearts with your love.

He gives strength to the weary and increases the power of the weak. Even youths grow tired and weary, and young men stumble and fall; but those who hope in the Lord will renew their strength.

Isaiah 40:29-31

Some days we can't go on. Some days even our physical strength has been pushed to the very limit. When we reach this point all we can do is place ourselves in God's hands and ask Him to strengthen us. He knows what we need. We must have the patience to rest in His arms until once more we can get up and walk on our own. It's human to grow weary. It is human to simply rest; until we have regained our strength enough to get up and take another step.

I Must Rest

Father, I cannot go on.
All my strength is spent.
Even now it is impossible
for me to lift my head to see your face.
At this moment I cannot
even bring my hands together in prayer.
Lord, as I lay here in your arms,
strengthen me body and soul.

FORGIVENESS

Jesus said,
"Father, forgive them,
for they do not know
what they are
doing."

Luke 23:34

Bear with each other and forgive whatever grievances you may have against one another. Forgive as the Lord forgave you.

Colossians 3:13

It is much easier to cling to anger than to forgive. It is far less difficult to hold those feelings within us, than to let them go and embrace our enemies. We know, however, we are all called to forgiveness. *"If we make our enemies our friends they will no longer be our enemies."* *If we are able to find a way to forgive those who have wronged us, we move one step closer to bringing peace not only into our own lives, but into the world.

* *Unknown source*

Father Forgive Them

Lord, please help me
with this anger I am feeling at this moment.
I know
that as you looked down from Your cross
upon those who crucified You,
You forgave them.
It is so painful for me
to forgive those who bring so much evil,
so much destruction upon this world.
Please help me Lord
to see others as You gazed at them from Your cross
with love, pity and compassion.
Most of all Lord,
help me to love others
with the same forgiving heart,
as when You spoke,
"Father forgive them."

Be kind and compassionate to one another.

Ephesians 4:32

Sometimes it is not easy to forgive those whom we love. How much more difficult is it than to forgive those whom we do not love as we should? It is a difficult task to move beyond our anger and offer forgiveness. Yet, this is the only way we can continue on our journey to the Kingdom. It is the only way we can free ourselves from the captive bonds of our unforgiving ness.

No Bounds

Forgive me Lord
for not being as forgiving
as I know I should be.
Your forgiveness toward your people,
even those who harmed You, knew no bounds.
Because of this,
You were free to move beyond
the suffering on your cross and return to our Father.
Help me Lord to forgive myself for not pardoning others,
so I may find the forgiveness in my heart
to love those who have hurt me,
who have injured those I love.
Lord, help me to loosen these chains of unforgiving ness
that keep me from freely returning to our Father.

Jesus answered, "I tell you, not seven times, but seventy-seven times.

Matthew 18:22

When asked by His Apostles how many times we must forgive those who hurt us, the number grew each time Jesus answered the question. The meaning was: as many times as we are wronged, that is the number of times we must forgive. It takes a great deal of courage to forgive someone for an act that hurts us. Several acts take much love and an abundance of grace.

More than Humanly Possible

Lord, you will have to help me
with this lesson you gave your Apostles.
I can forgive most people who hurt me once,
possibly twice,
but Lord seven times?
Then seven times seventy times?
Lord I hear your words,
I know what you are saying.
For You, I know it is possible.
I am human,
not such an easy task for me.
Lord only with your help
can I live this lesson of Forgiveness.
Forgiveness flows from your love,
let it reign through me,
so I may forgive as you ask,
even when it is more than humanly possible.

Yet the Lord longs to be gracious to you; He rises to show you compassion. For the Lord is a God of justice. Blessed are all who wait for Him!

Isaiah 30:18

Forgiveness does not take away justice. Forgiveness allows justice to be complete, to be fully executed. All who act against the law must be held accountable to it in this life, and ultimately will be held accountable in the next. It is this ultimate accountability that frees us when someone escapes accountability on earth. Part of being able to move through the process toward forgiveness is trusting that God will have the last word. He is the Alpha and the Omega, the beginning and the end. He dealt justly with man in the beginning, and He will deal justly with man in the end. What a burden this takes off our human shoulders. What a relief to know we can completely trust in God's ultimate justice, so we are freed to move to forgive all those who have acted wrongly against us.

Beginning to the End

Only you my God can deliver true justice,
justice that is unencumbered by the human emotions
imposed upon our existence.
I pray heavenly Father for the grace
to pass the deliverance of this justice that within
my own heart
wants to be imposed on my terms onto you.
Your ways are not my ways,
and to extract true justice I must let go,
I must forgive.
I must trust you God to do all you must do.
I trust you heavenly Father
to be the just One you have always been,
from the beginning to the end.

OUR BROTHERS AND SISTERS

"A *new command* I *give you*:
Love one another:
As I *have loved you*,
so you must love
one another."

John 13:34

"Therefore keep watch, because you do not know the day nor the hour."

Matthew 25:13

Jesus knew He was going to die in Jerusalem. He knew what was awaiting Him, and He prepared Himself in every way possible for that moment. Jesus took those last steps knowing what was at the end of them. Yet, how many take their steps each day with absolutely no idea when they will take their last. We do not know when we will take that last step upon this earth. Our hearts go out to all those who meet their deaths suddenly. We are saddened, because so many are walking through the veil of death before they have taken care of all the unfinished business in their lives.

Very Last Breath

Lord,
I pray for all those whom You have called from this life.
I pray for all those who had plans
to build larger grain bins to store their wealth, their goods.
Lord,
I pray for all those who were walking along enjoying the
world around them.
I pray
You allowed them to see Your face.
I pray
they took every opportunity to be a part of Your Kingdom.
We do not know how many final moments we have Lord
to call upon Your name, to feel Your love,
to ask Your forgiveness.
Because of Your mercy
we know not one soul will be left
without every possible opportunity to be saved,
even if it is the very last breath
we take upon this earth.

Let us fix our eyes on Jesus, the author and perfecter of our faith, who for the joy set before Him endured the cross.
                                                    Hebrews 12:2

Knowing how heavy our own crosses are at times, we can look at the crosses of others and better understand what they may be going through. We have even more compassion towards those who must carry a cross unjustly placed upon them by others, simply because they were in the wrong place at the wrong time. There are many souls who must carry these heavy crosses, simply because they are innocent victims.

Innocent Souls

Lord, please help me to understand
the crosses now being carried by those around me,
especially those
who have had crosses placed upon them
because of where their journeys may have taken them.
Lord, hear my prayer
for all the innocent souls
who now have crosses that seem almost impossible to bear.
Please Lord,
give all of these precious souls
the grace to persevere,
despite all that is now placed upon their shoulders.

Now may the Lord of peace himself give you peace at all times and in every way.

2 Thessalonians 3:16

It is difficult to understand why there are many in this world who do not desire peace or who believe peace only comes through violence or oppression. If we truly desire peace, it will only come through peace with one another. Yet before we can find peace with one another, we must first find it with God. We must allow Him to be the central part of our life. Only when we find true peace with our Creator can we be at peace with ourselves and those around us.

Peace follows the love that flows from our heart toward our Creator and our brothers and sisters. It is the only way towards true peace in this world and the next. We must pray at every possible moment for peace. We must pray for the Holy Spirit to enlighten the souls of the many who do not desire peace, or desire it only on their terms, not on the terms of the One who sends out His Spirit upon this earth.

Grant us Peace O Lord

Lord, as I look at the world around me,
as I see so many confused,
angry souls who are struggling at every turn,
I pray for peace O Lord.
Peace within me,
so I may bring this peace to others.
Your peace, brought through Your Holy Spirit.
I pray for peace O Lord.
Peace for those around me and far away from me.
Grant us peace O Lord,
before all those who do not desire peace
leave us with no peaceful days
upon this earth.

Peacemakers who sow in peace raise a harvest of righteousness.
James 3:18

Despite all the violence that has manifested itself around us, there is only one answer—to strive for peace, in whatever way possible. No matter how long a process it may be, we must continue toward the only solution that is lasting.

Lasting Peace

Lord,
please give me the strength and the perseverance
to strive for what is lasting.
Give me the courage to continue,
even when our human reaction
is to look toward other solutions.
I know Lord what You taught us
when you were with Your beloved Apostles.
Please Lord
help me to live by those teachings.

"But I tell you: Love your enemies and pray for those who persecute you."

Matthew 5:44

Those who commit violent acts against us and against society are still our brothers and sisters in Christ. Through the teachings of our Lord we are called to love them. We do not, nor should we, love their actions. But, the soul itself we must love, even as Christ loves us. These souls also need to be loved through our prayers. Our hearts are broken and hurt over their actions. Their hearts and more importantly their souls are lost. Our prayers are an important part of helping them.

Save Them Lord

I pray Lord
for all the souls who have lost their way.
Please help them Lord
in their darkness.
Bring them to your light
even though it be only a glimmer
seen at this moment through our prayers.
Bind the evil one Lord
who has taken over their souls,
show them your truth.
Save them Lord from the pit of destruction.
They are still our brothers and sisters,
though their actions
are far away from your love.

HOPE AND THANKSGIVING

*"I have told you these things,
so that in Me you may
have peace.
In this world you will
have trouble,
but take heart!
I have overcome the world."*

John 16:33

"Greater love has no one than this, that he lay down his life for his friends."

John 15:13

There is no greater gift than to give up one's life for one's brother. Most often we give our lives for others just short of shedding blood or actually dying for one another. At other times, however, we must answer that call even to the point of death. It is in this selfless act we see true love. It is also in this selfless act we see true hope.

Hope

So many Lord
experience the world around them crumbling.
So many even perish.
Despite the circumstances of their injuries or death,
there are many who come to their aid,
unmindful of the risk of injury or death to themselves.
It is in these selfless acts Lord I know You are there.
It is in these selfless acts Lord
we see Good rise above evil.
We have hope Lord
in seeing so many who are willing to give up their lives
for their brethren.
We have hope Lord
in seeing them give up all they possess,
because the only thing they truly possess is
love.
Thank you Lord for showing us this hope.

He will call upon Me, and I will answer him; I will be with him in trouble, I will deliver him and honor him.

Psalm 91:15

When tragedy hits close to our home, to our loved ones, or even to ourselves, it is a most difficult task to see the good in all that is going on around us. When the tragedy is brought about because of evil manifested through the acts of others, it is almost impossible to see anything but the evil itself. God allows what happens because He will not interfere with the free will of man. He plays no part in the evil itself, except to take the result of the evil action and turn it to good for the greater glory of His Kingdom. He will use every way possible to make this transformation possible. If we understand this, we can look at the situation and know there will be good that will come about because of it; then we can better accept any evil that may befall us.

The Hidden Good

Lord,
Sometimes I cannot understand
what is happening in this world,
or to those whom I love.
Yet I know You are all powerful,
You are compassionate and understanding.
Please Lord,
show us Your compassion and power
by bringing about goodness from such evil actions.
Help me Lord to see beyond the evil.
Help me Lord to see the hidden good
that can only be seen
through the power of Your love.

"And if I go and prepare a place for you, I will come back and take you to be with me, that you also may be where I am."

John 14:3

There is so much hope in this passage from John's gospel. There is so much hope in what awaits all of us. It doesn't make it any easier to say goodbye to those we love, but knowing our Lord will return to take all of us to Himself makes it a lot easier to accept. Knowing that those who have fallen asleep in Christ's peace have been escorted to the highest heavens gives us this unseen hope in what awaits all of us.

A Place Prepared for Us

Lord, it is disheartening to say goodbye,
just as it was for Your disciples,
Your beloved Apostles,
to say goodbye to You.
Yet, You made them a promise,
You said You would come back for them.
What hope Lord
we have in these words.
What hope Lord
we have in Your love for each one of us.
Thank you Lord
for preparing this place for us.
Thank you Lord
for giving us this hope, when all our hope
seemed to be so quickly taken away.

"So with you: Now is your time of grief, but I will see you again and you will rejoice, and no one will take away your joy."

John 16:22

It is inconceivable to imagine *joy* that can never be taken away when we have seen it disappear so quickly at the hands of those who hold no true joy in their hearts. It is as if someone has taken our breath from us. So very quickly we find ourselves gasping for air, when just a few seconds ago it was so plentiful. We cannot even imagine the joy we had before, when it is so suddenly taken away from us.

Everlasting Joy

Lord, I know that true joy fills my heart
only because of Your love.
I know that true joy only comes from You,
a joy that no one can take away.
Thank you Lord for this hope
You have given us in these words
spoken to Your Apostles.
So many today Lord cannot find this joy,
because they cannot find You.
Please dear Lord show them the hope
that awaits them beyond the grief,
beyond the sorrow.
Show them Lord the everlasting joy
that awaits all those who find You.

After Job had prayed for his friends, the Lord made him prosperous again and gave him twice as much as he had before.

Job 42:10

We know that just beyond the dark clouds there is clear blue sky and sunshine. We have faith that one day the clouds will pass and the sun will once more shine upon us. The clouds themselves keep us from enjoying the warmth of the sun, but we cannot let the clouds keep us from having hope that the sun is just behind their cover. As the days pass one by one and we see no break in the clouds, we still must continue to believe that very soon the sun will shine.

Beyond the Gray

Lord, dark clouds have closed in on me.
Blue that seemed so plentiful just a few days ago
has vanished.
I know Lord your rays of light
are still there beyond what is visible to me at this moment.
Thank you Lord for this hope.
Just as I know
that beyond the gray
of these clouds is the clear blue sky,
I also know that beyond the gray
of what has been placed upon this world
there is a new sunrise
just beginning to show itself
over the horizon.

"Hope that is seen is no hope at all. Who hopes for what he already has?"

Romans 8:24

It is contrary to reason to have hope in what is not seen when so much of what is seen in the world tries to snatch it away. Yet, as St. Paul reminds us: How can we go on hoping, if it is already seen? In this passage we clearly come to the understanding that we must continue despite what we may now be seeing in our lives. We must continue moving toward what is unseen, for that is where we shall see what we hope for.

Unseen Hope

It was easy to have hope Lord
when all I was seeing was pleasing to the eye.
When I could see the world without so much evil,
without so much violence,
I could easily hope for so much more.
Now Lord it is difficult.
Hope seems to be diminishing.
This is however when I must hope even more.
It is because of all that I am now seeing
that I place all my hope in what is unseen.
Thank you Lord for this unseen hope,
for all the glimpses you allow us to feel in our hearts,
and sometimes even see with our eyes.
Thank you Lord,
because You are our only
HOPE.

> *Then the end will come, when He hands over the kingdom to God the Father after he has destroyed all dominion, authority and power. For He must reign until he has put all His enemies under His feet.*
>
> 1 Corinthians 15:24-25

Evil will never triumph over *Good*. In the end, or what faithful Christians call "The beginning", it will be *Good* that will be the ultimate victor in this battle. It will be the Holy Spirit who will prevail over the spirit of evil, and it will be our Lord Jesus Christ who will escort His people home to our heavenly Father. Then our Lord will give to His Father the Kingdom that was built one soul at a time, souls who used their free wills for the greater glory of God and not the temporary illusion of glory through evil.

The Beginning

Come Lord Jesus,
come by the power of Your Holy Spirit.
Change the hearts
of those who do not recognize
Your truth,
Your love,
Your complete faithfulness
to Your people.

The triumph of the wicked has always been brief.

Job 20:5

But the word of the Lord remains for ever.

1 Peter 1:25

About the Cross

Initially, before Jesus' Resurrection the cross was looked at as something that meant the end. Jesus' death upon it changed all of that. His death and Resurrection put the cross in a totally different light. The cross would now be looked at as a sign of hope. It was now a sign of life.

While walking along the beach in Central California a few years before writing this book I stumbled upon the cross that was used for the image in this book. It was embedded in the sand, and by the appearance of the fresh seaweed wrapped around the two pieces of driftwood that made the cross; it was obvious it had just recently washed ashore. My friends, who were with me that day, were as amazed as I was upon finding this incredible gift.

The finding of this cross changed my life in ways that I would have never imagined. I carried this cross back to the house we were staying, and in spirit, have not stopped carrying it since. Yet, the carrying of this cross, although most difficult at times, has taught me many lessons: The most important one being: even though it appears each one of us carry our own cross, we never carry it alone. Our Lord is always there with us. No matter what happens while we journey with our Lord, we cannot worry about how others react to our calling to serve Him, or if they approve or disapprove of what our Lord asks of us. Each one of us must listen to the Spirit within our own hearts. If we choose to acknowledge and use the gifts He has bestowed upon us, He will show us the direction we are to take. I also came to an understanding that we are who we are. No matter how our life begins or what direction it takes, all of us have the ability to grow with the Lord. Despite our mistakes and failures we can rise above them. That is the gift God gave us through His Son's death upon the cross.

I left the cross I found that day at the home where we were staying that weekend. It was left behind so others could be touched by this wonderful gift from God. Despite leaving it behind, this cross continues to touch my life, and it will forever be a part of my journey.